Presented to:

____

From:

____

DARE TO LOVE

A 4 Week Devotional to help you love yourself and others.

BY D. C GOMEZ

Dare to Love
ISBN: 978-1-7333160-7-1 (Paperback)
Published by Gomez Expeditions
Request to publish works from this book should be sent to:
author@dcgomez-author.com

I dedicate *The Dare Collection* to my parents:

Two of the most passionate people I have ever met. They embrace life to the fullest. When life was full of challenges and difficulties, they focused on the positive side of things and finding humor in everything. Every adventure I have undertaken, they have been my greatest cheerleaders.

Thank you for loving life and sharing it

with everyone you meet.

INTRODUCTION

Have you ever noticed how often we use the word *love* in our everyday conversations and thoughts? It's that word we use loosely to describe every little thing we like or anything that moves us. Just today, I replied to several posts by saying how much I *love* ice cream, dragons, and *The Little Mermaid.* In the same time period, I told a friend how I *love* my nephews and couldn't wait to see them. Are all these the same type of love? Do we have different levels of love?

In the English language, love seems to be used for everything. As a native Spanish speaker, this was hard for me to understand. In Spanish, we have different words to express the different *types* of love. *"Te quiero"* is the phrase I would say to my family and close friends when I'm expressing my feelings towards them. "*Te amo*" is what we would say to a spouse, partner, or significant other. It's that deeper level of love that makes you crave and need the other person. Growing up, I rarely said "*te amo.*" It has such a strong passionate connection that it never seemed appropriate. The strange thing is I remember using the word *Love* (in English) more freely.

It's no wonder we're so confused and even afraid of love. Honestly, I like ice cream a lot, but I will survive if I can't have it anymore. My nephews are a whole different story. I love them. I'm willing to give up my life to protect them. In these twenty-eight days together, our goal is to explore the meaning of love. The love that would make you want to move mountains for others and makes us want to be better people.

This type of love for many of us is hard to imagine or even believe in. Probably because many of us have never seen it modeled for us. Unconditional love is not something we're used to, even with ourselves. But what if I told you true happiness comes from unconditional love? Would you believe me?

As we embark on this journey together, I hope you open your mind and heart to the possibility of love. To give yourself permission to believe you deserve to be happy and cherished. I pray you find the strength and determination to love for the sake of love and with no requirements or expectations.

LOVE
WEEK 1

THE TRUE MEANING OF LOVE

If you search the internet for the meaning of love, you will find answers like: "an intense feeling of deep affection, a great interest and pleasure in something, feel deep affection, like or enjoy very much." Sometimes, it feels like we don't have accurate words to describe the feeling. One thing is true: love can be a powerful motivator. Some philosophers believe love is the mightiest force in the world. Like any force, it can push us to accomplish great things. But when it's corrupted or tainted, we can do horrible things with the same intensity.

To ensure we are talking about the true meaning and power of love, I started with Saint Paul's definition found in I Corinthians thirteen. Many of us are very familiar with this scripture. They are some of the most used words for wedding vows all over the world. The truth behind them is that Paul never intended them for couples or weddings but as a guide for the new Christians in the city of Corinth in Greece.

As we explore his words, imagine how different the world would be if we all treated each person we met with this type of love. To love others, and ourselves, with absolute patience and compassion each day. This type of love would transform the world. This week we will reflect on specific segments of this scripture and examine the meaning of love in the way the apostle actually wanted us to.

DAY 1

And if I have the gift of prophecy and comprehend all mysteries and all knowledge; if I have all faith so as to move mountains but do not have love, I am nothing. (1 Corinthians 13:2)

How many times have we wished we were smarter or maybe more talented? I know I have. I even prayed to have more faith, to be the believer who could handle everything that came to me just by the power of my faith. The interesting thing is, according to Paul, those things are worthless. Even if we had the gift to predict the future to improve our lives, without love, everything is meaningless. Humans without love, based on Paul's beliefs, are nothing.

Paul's words are powerful and even controversial. If you're familiar with the New Testament, you've probably seen the theme of love spread throughout the text. Paul, among many other apostles, truly believed that loving one another was one of the most important things we could do. One reason is because many scholars believe Jesus came down to earth to teach people how to love. Even during the times of Jesus, people were disrespectful and hateful towards each other. It focused Paul on spreading Jesus's message—to love one another.

Let's put this into perspective. It doesn't matter how intelligent or talented you are. If you don't have love to receive or give, your days will lack meaning and purpose. We are meant to live in communion with each other. A community where people love and care for each other and respect each other every day.

Reflection Time

How is your relationship with the people around you? Do you treat them all the same, or do you treat some better than others based on their status?

DAY 2

"If I give away everything I own, and if I hand my body over so that I may boast but do not have love, I gain nothing." (1 Corinthians 13:3)

Paul was not known for holding his tongue. He was not afraid to speak his mind and tell people the truth. This scripture is a splendid example of Paul's ability to share the truth. He's speaking here to all the hypocrites of his time. Those individuals that pride themselves on all their good deeds and acts of hardship, but their intentions were lacking. They're not sacrificing themselves for their love of others, but for praise and recognition.

It is not enough to "do" good. That goodness we accomplished must be felt in our soul. We need to feel love and compassion for those we're serving. Our goal is to look at others with eyes of love, not judgment or boastfulness, to serve and care for others while expecting nothing in return.

In a culture of immediate gratification, it's hard to give and sacrifice with no expectations and to be present and helping in the moment with an open heart has become very difficult. Because in the end, as Paul reminds us, we gain nothing if we don't do everything with love.

Love makes every sacrifice worthwhile.

Reflection Time

Many of us know influential organizations that are doing well in our communities. Many of them are always in search of volunteers or even monetary support. Can you find an organization in your community that you can support anonymously? Give for the sake of giving.

DAY 3

"Love is patient, love is kind. It is not jealous, [love] is not pompous, it is not inflated." (1 Corinthians 13:4)

When I first read this scripture, it honestly didn't seem that hard to follow. That all changed when I fell in love for the first time. I was never a jealous person before, but the green-eyed-monster would come out when my boyfriend at the time would rather go out with his friend than spend time with me. Without trying, I bragged about myself to get his attention. I was in a constant state of competition, and I was never truly happy.

Later in my life, I blamed my insecurity for that behavior. What I discovered was that it went deeper than that. I didn't know how to love. To love another person and have patience as they went through their own journey was hard. Sometimes we don't feel kind. When we're hurting, we hurt others, even without meaning to.

What Paul is asking of us is to be patient. To be kind and supportive of every person who we have in our lives. Imagine being in a relationship where people don't have to brag or compete for attention. Healthy loving relationships are ones where people are given room to grow and feel supported. These traits can be hard at first if we aren't used to expressing them, but they can be cultivated and grown. We can all learn to be much more patient and compassionate with each other.

Reflection Time

Analyze the relationships in your life. Which ones are flourishing? Which ones are a constant struggle? Could you focus today on being a little more forgiving and patient with those individuals in your life that have a way of irritating you?

DAY 4

"It [love] is not rude, it does not seek its own interest, it is not quick-tempered, it does not brood over injury." (1 Corinthians 13:5)

It is easy to see why couples use this scripture so often for their vows. It's a glorious reminder to not disrespect your partner and to protect their feelings. But remember, Paul wrote this for a community. His goal was to teach the Corinthians how to treat each other as a member of the body of Christ. To respect one another and not to put their own feelings above others.

Paul goes one step further in his explanation. He adds that love doesn't get angry easily. Let's be honest, many of us are quick to jump to conclusions and explode when people do us wrong. Paul urges the Corinthians, as well as us, to avoid keeping a record of other's transgressions. While we claim to forgive people, the moment they make us mad we're quick to bring back their past. We don't let go of their mistakes. Instead we hold on to them and dwell on the pain.

Unconditional love is not focused on causing harm to others. If we weren't hurt or suffering, would we even try to hurt others? By not keeping a record or getting angry easily, we avoid filling our souls with resentment and pain. A heart free of hatred and hurt can be filled with joy and love. By wanting only good for those around us, can our love grow?

Reflection Time

We have all been hurt at one point in our lives. Can you think of a person who has done you wrong, and have you forgiven them? Are you keeping a record of their transgressions, even if you don't bring them up? What is holding you back from letting go?

DAY 5

"It [love] does not rejoice over wrongdoing but rejoices with the truth." (1 Corinthians 13:6)

Many of us have heard the saying, "the truth will set you free." This is a powerful model to live by. It encourages people to live a life of honesty, not only with other people but with themselves. It is extremely difficult to keep up with a lie. Not only do you have to remember it, you must create more lies to support the initial one. All of this is exhausting to your soul. It is hard to fill ourselves with love when we're busy trying to keep up with the lies we've told.

The same goes with living a life full of strife and discord. We've all met people who enjoy causing drama. They gain pleasure by seeing others suffer. As Paul states, if you love someone or if your heart is full of love for people, you will not enjoy these things. You will work hard to create an environment around you where people are kind and respectful daily.

We all have options in our lives. How we react to things is the only thing we can truly control. We can break the cycle of evil and help those around us feel loved and understood. Love can spread as quickly as any pandemic if we let it ignite in our souls.

Reflection Time

Make a pact with yourself today to only speak the truth when necessary. You will decide that you will be an agent of change in your community by not spreading rumors about others. Just because it's the truth, it does not have to be shared with the world.

DAY 6

"It [love] bears all things, believes all things, hopes all things, endures all things." (1 Corinthians 13:7)

It would be easy to dismiss the words of Paul as just merely a dream. To see them as pretty sayings to inspire us. Paul did more than preach; he lived the lessons he taught. He wrote many of his letters from a jail cell. Even under persecution and threat for his life, Paul still loved his enemies. He loved the new Christians he was trying to guide. Paul gave love to everybody he met, enemies and allies alike.

In some of his letters, Paul defended those who had made mistakes, and even asked for their forgiveness from the law. With his background in mind, it's easy to see why Paul urges us to remember to always hope and preserve. In this simple line, Paul provides us with instructions on how to live our lives and express our love to those around us. His message and descriptions are action steps that we can all take.

They're difficult. When we've been hurt, it's hard to trust and have faith in others. It's hard to protect strangers in a society that keeps telling us to watch out for criminals. When things are not going well, it's hard to believe that love will never fail. But these are choices we all must make. We can choose to focus on the negative, or we can find the positive in every situation. If we can change our perspective, then the view will always improve.

Reflection Time

Take a few moments to make a list of all the areas in your life you feel aren't going well. Now analyze each one of them and see which one you can change that might change your perspective. What thing is going well in that area? Can you focus on that?

DAY 7

"Love never fails. So faith, hope, love remain, these three; but the greatest of these is love." (1 Corinthians 13:8, 13)

We've made it to the seventh day, my friend, and this is the perfect scripture to wrap up our week. Paul brings it all together with this glorious reminder. Love is the greatest thing we should have. Love binds everything together, giving shape to our faith and our hope.

This week we explored Paul's beautiful description of love, a love so deep and powerful it would forgive anything, conquer anything, and endure all. The key for growing our love is it needs to be something we practice with everyone, including ourselves. Love motivates us to treat everyone with patience, kindness, and honor. Can you imagine a world where every person was accepted just because they were human? This is the power of love. When we love others, we only want the best for them.

Reflect on the power of these three things: faith, hope, and love. If you knew you could never fail, what would you dare to do? Living in a place of love will fill your heart with joy and hope. Mistakes would never seem like failures but lessons we learned on our way to greatness.

Reflection Time

Paul's definition of love is more action steps. Pick one that best moves you and find a way to apply it in your everyday life. The more we practice loving one and another, the more it becomes part of our nature.

CONGRATULATIONS MY FRIEND!

I am so excited for you. We have completed our first week together on this journey to understand and improve our own idea of love. During this week, we explored the definition and expectation of love according to Saint Paul. Love goes outside traditional relationships and should be extended to people in our circle as well as outside of it. We can be kind, patient, and understanding with anyone we meet without being defensive.

When we choose to put our egos aside and not worry about defending our pride, we can have more compassion for other people every day. If we expand our love beyond our immediate family to those we meet, we can create a ripple effect around the world. As Paul states, love never fails, love conquers all, love forgives all.

Week 1 – Reflection Time

As we wrap up Week One, take a couple of minutes to reflect on the scriptures and any thoughts, emotions, or patterns that arose during your journey. Did you agree with Paul's guidance or did it seem too hard? What is something that surprised you this week?

WEEK 2

LOVING OTHERS

Throughout our history, we have seen many cases of individual selfless acts. They have put the welfare of others before their own. This is due in part to the love they have for their fellow human beings. Some people are born with this innate ability to love and care without reservation. Many of us have to learn it and practice it as we grow. The good news is, our mindset towards others can always change.

We can all develop an attitude of understanding and appreciation toward others. Our love for our fellow members of this world might not hit Mother Teresa's proportion, but it doesn't have to. We don't have to sacrifice our lives like Gandhi or even Martin Luther King Jr. All we are asked to do is those little things Paul described to the people of Corinthians: do not dishonor, do not delight in evil, and don't be envious.

As we start week two, we will explore the scriptures and expand our understanding on how to be loving towards others. It's easy to be gentle to those who we are in relations with. It's a whole unique situation to still show love to those we have done wrong. I urge you to keep an open heart, and let this week inspire you to find love and understanding for everyone you meet.

DAY 8

Laban replied, "I prefer to give her to you rather than to an outsider. Stay with me." So Jacob served seven years for Rachel, yet they seemed to him but a few days because of his love for her.
(Genesis 29:19-20)

For many of us, when we think of love towards others, the first people we think about are our significant others or immediate family. They're usually dear to our heart and at the top of our mind. This scripture is an outstanding example to describe the sacrifices we will make for the people we love. Jacob was head over heels for Rachel. He loved her so much that he would work for her dad for seven years just for her hand in marriage.

In a culture that needs things to happen now, waiting seven years for a person might feel like an eternity. But as Paul explained, love is patient. When we're deciding with our eyes of love, we'll endure anything. We're willing to sacrifice our comfort for the happiness of others.

The beautiful part is when we're in love, it doesn't feel like a sacrifice. Jacob states it really well with her. While he worked for seven years, to him it only felt like a few days. Love will change the way we approach things. We are more willing to do more for others while expecting nothing in return.

Reflection Time

Think of the people in your life. Is there a situation where you could put that person's needs before yours? What is one thing you could do to make that person's day a little easier?

DAY 9

"When the day came for Elkanah to offer sacrifice, he used to give a portion each to his wife Peninnah and to all her sons and daughters, but a double portion to Hannah because he loved her, though the Lord had made her barren." (1 Samuel 1:4-5)

In the Old Testament, for a woman to be barren was a great dishonor to her husband and herself. This was something that everyone looked down upon. For Elkanah to overlook this and show extra favor to his wife for her suffering was a very progressive action. He did it because of love. I can only imagine the criticism he received for his initiative, yet he continued to do it.

In our current times, how do we show our love to the people in our lives that we claim to care for? Many people claim to love their significant others, yet they talk down to them. They create strife in their home and maintain tension. They validate their actions because they provide monetary security, but their partners don't feel loved and are constantly disrespected.

It is not enough to tell others we love them. Actions are just as important. We should show them how special they are and that we care. This could require a mindset change to not take them for granted.

Reflection Time

Every day we have an opportunity to show the people in our lives that we care. Today, take a few moments to show that special person how much you care for them. Do something special for them that they normally wouldn't expect.

DAY 10

"He will be your comfort and the support of your old age, for his mother is the daughter-in-law who loves you. She is worth more to you than seven sons!" (Ruth 4:15)

Taking care of the people we have fallen in love with is a natural thing for many of us. Helping our family when they're in need is not a far-fetched idea to imagine. The real question is are we willing to provide the same level of loving care for those we have no responsibility for? Ruth did just that for her mother-in-law, Naomi, after their husbands passed away. Naomi had told Ruth to head back to her own city and leave her. Ruth refused.

Reflect on the scripture above. Naomi's neighbor compared Ruth to Naomi's sons. That was huge. Back in those days, men had a higher status than woman. Naomi's husband and sons were killed in battle (including Ruth's husband). Naomi was alone, an old woman, and destitute, with nothing to give back to anyone. Ruth didn't care. She followed Naomi back to Israel and worked twice as hard to support them both.

Love goes beyond blood or family. It can transcend circumstances and give us the will to tackle all things for the people in our lives. When we express our love to others, people around us take notice and will be inspired by it.

Reflection Time

Has someone inspired you to do something more than you could imagine? Write about any situation where love has moved you to do something more than you thought possible.

DAY 11

"The covetous man is never satisfied with money, and the lover of wealth reaps no fruit from it; so this too is vanity." (Ecclesiastes 5:9)

We've been talking about the power of love that moves us to do good and the motivation it gives us to help those in our lives. But like Ecclesiastes points out, the love for money can also have consequences. Sometimes those consequences don't end up being positive ones. For the greedy man, pursuing money doesn't end, not even when they have plenty of it. The desire to have more money usually comes at the expense of those around them.

We have all seen people willing to stab others in the back to climb the corporate ladder. Or the professionals that ignore their family in search of the next promotion. What many of these people have in common is they end up alone and sometimes miserable. Many started working long hours to support their loved ones. Unfortunately, at some point they get a taste for power and money, and that initial goal gets twisted and corrupted.

Working hard and achieving great things is a blessing we can all rejoice in. But when the intentions of our hearts are focused on power and our egos, the results are not always the most honorable. Don't lose sight of why you started working those long hours. Don't take for granted the people who love you. The people in your life will motivate you. Keep them at the front of your thoughts.

Reflection Time

We all have areas in our lives we can work on improving. What can you do in the next seven days to help you be more focused on people and less on material possessions?

DAY 12

"But rather, love your enemies and do good to them, and lend expecting nothing back." (Luke 6:35)

Love your enemies is one of the hardest instructions in all the Bible, at least in my opinion. Jesus is asking us to be compassionate, patient, respectful, and helpful towards people who have done us wrong. It's easy to love pleasant people. Loving, or even just being friendly toward those who have never shown us any respect, is a challenge. How can we get there?

The key is in the second half of the scripture above. To lend, or in our case, to do something expecting nothing back. When we take away our expectations, we free ourselves from emotional attachment. We let go of the things we think we deserve and are never disappointed when we receive nothing in return.

My mother is an outstanding role model in this area. She helps everyone regardless of her personal relationship with them. It doesn't matter what they need; she is always the first one to assist. Her motto is, "do good and don't worry who they are." It's a very freeing way to live. To treat everyone with the same respect, and to share your gifts with all just because you can. It's the joy of showing love around the world. The best part is everything you put out into the universe will come back to you.

Reflection Time

Do you have a person, or maybe a group of people, who you harbor ill feelings toward? Can you look at them through eyes of love? Are you willing to forgive them?

DAY 13

[Jesus] said to him, "Feed my sheep. Amen, amen, I say to you, when you were younger, you used to dress yourself and go where you wanted; but when you grow old, you will stretch out your hands, and someone else will dress you and lead you where you do not want to go."
(John 21:17-18)

We talked about showing our love to those nearest and also to our enemies. In today's scripture, Jesus encouraged us to go one step further and show love to those who cannot do anything for us. One group he focuses on are the elderly. He asks us to remember that we will all grow old, and eventually we will need help ourselves. This is a very humbling thought.

By cultivating a spirit of love and compassion for those around us, we won't be upset when our help is needed. We will be glad to help our seniors and show them honor. Remember back in week one, "love don't dishonor." We're all in communion together. Some of us were not raised in a household that revered the old age. Instead, it was something that was looked down upon. In turn, that makes the seniors feel less than human.

We can change this behavior. We have the power to create new mindsets. To reprogram ourselves to see the world from a loving perspective. To cherish getting old and embrace the grace that comes with age and wisdom.

Reflection Time

Take a moment to write ten things you can only achieve as you get older. Take your time to explore the things we can only achieve with age. By focusing on the positive side of aging, it will start changing our perceptions to aging.

DAY 14

"No one has greater love than this, to lay down one's life for one's friends." (John 15:13)

When I first joined the military two decades ago, this was the scripture I played in my mind over and over. Yes, without a doubt, I would lay down my life for my friends and family. I was in Basic training on September 11, 2001 when the US was turned upside down. I knew then that I was willing to die to protect the constitution of the US. With the potential threat of war, the idea of dying for total strangers became an actual possibility.

As soldiers, they forced us to battle with this question every day. To lay down our freedom to defend the constitution of the United States and millions of people we don't even know. What if you had never served? Can you give up your life for others? Unconditional love is always the reason we would. Our subconscious mind will bypass reasons for love and help us do the most unthinkable things.

As you ponder on the people in your life that you hold dear, ask yourself what you are willing to do for them. If you aren't willing to sacrifice anything for them, take a minute to reevaluate the definition of love. Are you holding anything against them? Whatever those things are that you're holding against them, it's time to let them go.

Reflection Time

Take a few minutes to write your list of close friends and family members. From that list, look at the ones you're willing to make sacrifices for without needing too many details. From the ones that are left over, ask yourself what is holding you back. Remember, some people we can love from afar. Not everyone in our lives has our best interest at heart. Love them, respect them, but don't let yourself be used by them.

CONGRATULATIONS MY FRIEND,

Hope you are feeling as excited as I am. You have completed Week Two in this devotional. This is such a tremendous accomplishment for us. It is difficult to reflect on our lives, and it is definitely difficult to examine our perceptions and ideas of love. As we continue down this road, remember to be patient with yourself and those around you. We all have been through many difficult situations and have been programmed to believe a certain way about others and ourselves.

Our goal together is to redefine your idea of love, and to help you bridge the gap between those individuals in your life. Take your time as you continue to explore this definition and how it's expressing itself in your life. Don't be afraid if things feel a little strange or even hard. It can take us time to change, grow, and evolve. Keep an open heart and know you are on the right path to self-healing and love.

Week 2 – Reflection Time

As we wrap up week two, take some time to think of some things that popped out at you during the week. What were some of the most shocking revelations that came to you? Spend some time analyzing the scriptures and your notes throughout the week. Write how you truly feel about the concept of loving others.

WEEK 3

LOVING OURSELVES

The older I got, the more I realized I had a hard time being kind to myself. Loving others has always been a lot easier for me than it was to love me fully, with all of my insecurities and deficiencies. I've always been too hard on myself, and I hold myself to a higher standard in everything I do. Without a doubt, I'm notorious for setting unrealistic expectations. Rarely did I celebrate my accomplishments like I did others. Instead, I focused on everything that went wrong with my own goals.

I would never treat others with such a harsh attitude, so why did I treat myself so badly? Probably because, like many people, I was programmed to believe that in order to be a good person; I needed to be humble and never brag about myself. I needed to work hard and put everyone else first. As a result, I became a secondary character in my own life story.

Unfortunately, because I didn't know how to love myself, it made it difficult to love others fully. I didn't know how to love the "me" with the extra pounds, the "me" who made mistakes, or the "me" who failed. Overall, I didn't find myself to be deserving of compliments or even gifts. This translated to a damaged self-image with constant insecurities.

Thanks to the Lord, all this changed when I allowed myself to find love for me. Focus deep in my own eyes and see the wonderful, beautiful creation the Lord had made. This week, we're going to explore that concept: loving ourselves even when we don't think we deserve it.

DAY 15

"God created man in his image, in the divine image he created him; male and female he created them." (Genesis 1:27)

What better way to start week three than with Genesis, the first book in the Bible? For those who believe in a higher power, Genesis validates our existence. We were made by the most holy one to be just like him. The Lord decided we were so important to him that he didn't copy a cow or a monkey to create us. He took his own image and imprinted on us.

I know this belief goes in direct contradiction to our society and the theory of evolution. My goal is not to argue against it. In fact, I believe science and faith can coexist in order to explain the mysteries of life. Faith and spirituality fill in the gap science sometimes can't explain or leaves us questioning. To this day, modern medicine knows less than twenty percent of what our brains can do. Even without their validation or approval, humans are still functioning and thriving.

With that in mind, we can say to ourselves that God made us in his image, not just Adam. This means there is something special about us. There is something that goes beyond the science, cells and atoms. We're full of his love that is dying to express itself each day. Maybe it's time for us to treat his greatest creation with more patience and kindness. Maybe it's a great day to rejoice in the mystery that is our creation.

Reflection Time

Make a list of all the things you can do for yourself today. Don't judge your list, don't limit your ideas based on your circumstance. Just write all the things that make you smile. Then for the next seven days, pick one thing out of your list to splurge on. The goal is to show your own inner child how much you love them.

DAY 16

"So be perfect, just as your heavenly Father is perfect."
(Matthew 5:48)

Do you believe the Lord makes mistakes? If you believe that our heavenly father created the universe, is holding the world in place, and can maintain all forms of life; how could he possibly make a mistake with us? At times, we treat ourselves like our creation was an accident. That we were placed on this earth by chance, and that there is nothing good about us.

It is very difficult to love, or even to have compassion for something we think is substandard. We have a hard time seeing the perfection in ourselves. There are fifty trillion cells in our bodies, each one working in harmony for one goal: to keep us alive. Some of us struggle to be in relationships with five people, yet our bodies have mastered the ultimate perfection, life.

Why are we so hard on ourselves? We continue to look down on our own bodies. We pass judgment on our failures and even our successes. Rarely do we give ourselves credit for doing our best. Life is a brief journey, but it can be a very long, miserable ride when we go against ourselves. As the scripture states, we are perfectly made because the Lord made us in his image, and he is perfect.

Reflection Time

Today, start a new list. This one should include all the things you like about yourself. Every day add one more thing to this list. It doesn't matter how small you think it is. The goal is to always continue growing and appreciating everything you are.

DAY 17

"Your adornment should not be an external one: braiding the hair, wearing gold jewelry, or dressing in fine clothes, but rather the hidden character of the heart, expressed in the imperishable beauty of a gentle and calm disposition." (1 Peter 3:3-4)

In our society, it always feels like we're competing with the model on the magazines or the movie stars on the screen. We torture our bodies to become a certain way. When those expectations fail, we beat ourselves up for not measuring up. No wonder we have a hard time loving who we are right now. Many people plan to love and appreciate themselves when they reach a certain milestone: weight loss, finish school, get married—you can fill in the blanks.

Today's scripture helps us refocus our attention on what really matters. Instead of spending hours working on our exterior, we should work on the inside. The scriptures ask us to develop our character. To become gentler and calmer, which in turn will make us more loving. But it's not enough to be gentle with others. We should practice this trait with ourselves every day.

Next time you see yourself in the mirror and feel the desire to beat yourself up for not being a certain way, stop. Know you are doing your best. The outside will reflect on your soul and intentions. Develop those each day. Know that our bodies will change with time, but we will continue to be a perfect creation from the inside out.

Reflection Time

Have you ever talked down to yourself? Examine the conversations you're having with yourself, can you change the dialogue? Can you talk to yourself more loving in a way that better reflects the relationship you want to have with a best friend?

DAY 18

"You are all-beautiful, my beloved, and there is no blemish in you." (Song of Songs 4:7)

Telling the people in my life they're beautiful and that I love them is second nature to me. I don't have to think about it too much. It just comes naturally. The looks on their faces are priceless. Anytime I give them a compliment, they brighten and reflect so much joy. Then why couldn't I see the same beauty in myself?

A few years ago, I was told to complete a simple exercise: to stare in the mirror each day for one week and tell myself that I was beautiful, talented, and a magnificent creation of God. Some days I felt like I was lying. But by the seventh day, I could see myself and smile. I was grateful for the girl glancing back at me. Amazed at everything she went through and still how strong she was. Those words were true every day.

Now I can face the mirror and say, "Good morning, you good-looking girl." My entire demeanor has changed, and I giggle with joy. If nobody gives me a compliment, I will do it myself. Why not? Even the scriptures remind us we are beautiful and without blemish. We're not an accident, but a beautiful creation that should be cherished and rejoiced.

Reflection Time

I challenge you to take the same little exercise. As you are writing all the things you like about yourself, say them out loud in front of the mirror. It is time to reprogram our minds, and it starts with the words you speak to yourself. Go ahead, my friend, and make friends with your own soul.

DAY 19

"He who gains intelligence is his own best friend; he who keeps understanding will be successful." (Proverbs 19:8)

Often, we seek approval from exterior sources. We work really hard to impress those around us, to make the people in our lives proud. What if today's scriptures were right? What if we develop our own internal compass, or talents and skills and become our own best friends? How different our lives would be.

We wouldn't be so judgmental of ourselves, and instead we'd become our own personal cheerleaders. Just like we are for the people we love. We will become supportive, understanding, and always the first ones to give a word of encouragement when things go bad. This is not about being selfish but having a healthy self-image. The scriptures ask us to love our enemies like we love ourselves. Some people treat their enemies better than they do themselves.

In order to develop our self-love, first we must see ourselves as important. We need to see ourselves with the same eyes of caring as we see those we're in love with. At the core of our heart, we must believe we are our own best friend, who deserves to be nourished, protected, and cared for. Those are pretty big things if we've been neglecting who we are for a very long.

Reflection Time

The longest relationship we will ever have is the one we have with ourselves. What can you do to develop a more loving relationship with yourself? How can you treat yourself better today?

DAY 20

"Do you not know that you are the temple of God, and that the Spirit of God dwells in you? If anyone destroys God's temple, God will destroy that person; for the temple of God, which you are, is holy."
(1 Corinthians 3:16-17)

The first time I read this passage, it took me a minute to digest it. I've heard that our bodies are temples and we should take care of them. The last part of Paul's explanation to the Corinthians was the segment I was taking for granted. As Paul explained, our bodies are more than just temples; they are holy. This is a vast difference.

Think about this. If we treated our bodies as holy, we would worship them every day. We would thank them for all the sacrifices they have made for us. We would show them our love and worthiness and feed them only the best food around. Every day, we would make sure our temples are in the best condition, clean and dressed to impress. Like every temple should be.

Unfortunately, how often do we neglect our health? Many of us keep extremely busy schedules, with high stress and long hours. We don't sleep enough or feed our temples with the most nutritious food. It is a miracle how well our bodies take care of us considering all the abuse we put them through. We should love ourselves more and improve our relationship with our bodies.

Reflection Time

Based on the idea of your body being a temple, what is one habit you could change to improve your health? Take the time to reflect on your current habits and conditions and how you can improve them. Make a conscious analysis of all the things that are no longer serving you, and things you can do to feel better.

DAY 21

"I praise you, so wonderfully you made me; wonderful are your works!" (Psalms 139:14)

Today, my friend, I want us to recap the essence of who we are. As the scripture states, we were wonderfully made. The Lord only creates in two ways: perfectly and abundantly. Then we should never question that we were made in his perfection. Regardless of what our physical conditions look like, the Lord placed us on this earth to experience the magic of life. We were brought here to discover what it means to be human and have an incredible adventure.

We can enjoy our journey with passion and excitement by embracing who we are. Let's give ourselves room to grow, to learn, and even to fail. As we explore in week one, we can use all the elements of love to become more patient, gentle, and understanding with our own growth. Do not jump to conclusions or beat yourself up when things don't go exactly as planned. It's okay to have goals and expectations, but we don't have to become attached to them or their results. If we are open to what the universe will bring us, sometimes the results will be better than we expected.

Give yourself a mission, my friend, to love the beautiful self you are. You are worthy, you're talented, and you deserve to be cherished. Every day might not be incredible, but we can find one thing worthy of celebrating. Remember, you're wonderfully and perfectly made.

Reflection Time

How are you planning to celebrate the end of this week? Can you think of four things or five that you can do to show yourself love in a very special? Go ahead, be creative and enjoy the beauty of life.

CONGRATULATIONS MY FRIEND!

Give yourself a high five, my friend. Exploring self-love, how to develop it, and how to be kind to ourselves is hard work. Most of us don't truly see how hard we push ourselves. We also don't see the amount of stress we put our bodies through. This week was a brilliant start to open up that dialogue. To help us explore where we are in our own development.

This is just the beginning. I recommend continuing to practice affirmation words and phrases each day with yourself. To start a gratitude journal of all the things that are going well in your life. Be proud of your achievements and celebrate all the lessons you learn. This means you tried, and you were brave enough to take a chance.

Like any relationship, the one we develop with ourselves will grow overtime. This is something we continue to practice. Don't be afraid to explore the areas that are uncomfortable in your life, then forgive yourself. Release the pain and open your soul for healing and unconditional love.

Week 3 – Reflection Time

During week three, did anything jump out that surprised you? What were some things you were not aware of that you were holding back from yourself? Take a few minutes to explore these thoughts and see how you can start healing yourself in these areas.

WEEK 4

LOVING LIKE GOD-LIVING IN PEACE

Welcome, my friend, to our last week together in this devotional. I'm thrilled you want to continue on your journey to healing. Finding time for ourselves in our fast-paced culture can be challenging. But we truly need the time in order to let go of the past programming and pains we bring ourselves.

This week, in my opinion, is one of the hardest to process and believe in. God's love is one of the most complicated ones to understand. The idea of unconditional love is not something natural for us. We rarely see unconditional love shown in our everyday affairs. Love that forgives everything, holds no grudges, understands all, and only wants the good for others is hard to believe. Love for the sake of love, with nothing in return, is something we don't see every day.

If we are honest with ourselves, most of us have conditions for others. We were raised in households with conditions. Our parents were happy or proud as long as we did the right thing or made the right grades. As adults, we give our love to others as long as they are nice to us or provide something in return. This is the way our society has brought us to understand our conditions.

Our goal now is to transcend those things. To learn to love others, and especially ourselves, without conditions. We want to use some of those examples from the Lord to create healthier images of love and express it. Many of us are afraid to love because we feel it will not be reciprocated. This week let's see how God's love is, even when it is not returned to Him.

DAY 22

"He will love and bless and multiply you; he will bless the fruit of your womb and the produce of your soil. You will be blessed above all people." (Deuteronomy 7:13,14)

From the earlier books in the Old Testament, the Lord made commitments to his people. Over and over, he blessed them. He restated his covenant, to love them and to multiply them. The Lord wanted to make them a great nation above all. For those who believe God is all-powerful and all-knowing, this means God knows what his people are going to do before they do it. There are no surprises to God; he sees infinite possibilities in our future. Yet, even knowing all of this, he still loves us. The Lord continues to make covenants with his people.

Imagine someone promising you unlimited wealth and abundance beyond your imaginations for nothing in return besides genuine love. Would you believe them? In today's culture, we have a hard time believing in many offers. Our theory is if it's too good to be true, it probably is. This is the reason we don't believe in love. How can we believe that someone will love and give us anything our heart desires just because they feel like it?

Don't feel bad, my friend. For generations, the Israelites have been fighting the Lord's love and covenant. Probably because it sounded too good to be true. We're meant to be blessed. We're meant to be happy. For generations, the Lord has promised his blessings. It is time for us to reach for them and embrace them.

Reflection Time

What is your definition of unconditional love? Do you believe it's possible to love wanting nothing in return? Take a few moments to explore the idea of loving someone even if they don't love you back.

DAY 23

"Understand, then, that the Lord, your God, is God indeed, the faithful God who keeps his merciful covenant down to the thousandth generation toward those who love him and keep his commandments."
(Deuteronomy 7:9)

In the Old Testament, the Lord of Israel appeared as a jealous and vengeful God. Probably because people couldn't get things together. The Lord would liberate them from oppression, and then they would go back to sinning. It was a constant struggle for the chosen people. The prophets that were raised by God tried to guide them, but the people continued to worship false idols.

In the scripture above, this was another reminder to the people of God's faithfulness to them. For thousands of generations, the Lord would keep his covenant. He would continue to bless them and love them. Even with this promise of love, the people still do not believe and failed to love him back.

Let's be honest, I don't know if I am holy enough to forgive a person a thousand times. I would like to believe I don't hold grudges, but this struggle would drive me nuts. My goal is to take inspiration from the Lord. Even when the Bible describes God as a vengeful God, he was still faithful to his children. The Lord forgave over and over, regardless of whether the people deserved it. He believed they could be better and gave them a chance to find his love and live a blessed life.

Reflection Time

As we reflect on the scriptures for today, can you think of the people in your life who you are committed to? Reflect on your relationships with them. Are they based on mutual love, or does it feel you are always giving more? If so, is this out of love or because you expect something back?

DAY 24

Jesus answered and said to him, "Whoever loves me will keep my word, and my Father will love him, and we will come to him and make our dwelling with him." (John 14:23)

There is a drastic shift between the Old Testament and the New Testament. The message transition from fearing God to loving him. This shift was so radical that, in the New Testament, it changed the focus of the commandments. Jesus stated that the greatest commandment was to love God with all your heart. The theme of love continues with him saying, the second commandment is to love your neighbor like yourself.

Reading the scripture today, it should not surprise us when Jesus told us how his father would love us. Here's the beautiful thing about love. When we care for a person, we will do everything in our power to make them happy. We wouldn't want to hurt them or mistreat them. When we join in a relationship of love with the Lord, keeping his word is easy. But we know he only wants to bless us and increase our world with his blessings.

This is a type of love we should have for ourselves and those in our lives. The type that wants everyone to succeed. Love so big that it benefits everyone in that relationship, not just one person. This type of love can be cultivated and harvested. All we have to do is be open to it and willing to practice it each day.

Reflection Time

In what areas of your life can you work to ensure that the relationships you have are open and understanding? How can you benefit from those around you by sharing your love without questions?

DAY 25

"With age-old love I have loved you; so I have kept my mercy toward you." (Jeremiah 31:3)

The scriptures for today have a very romantic feel. The phrase "age-old love" conjures images of timeless love affairs that surpass significant obstacles. To some extent, this is probably true. The love of the Lord has been a love story that transcends time and space. He has loved his children from the beginning of time and continues to do so. This is incredible love and the reason he gives us his mercy without asking. To forgive our faults every day, even when we don't deserve, it, is incredible.

An age-old love should be a great long-term goal to have with ourselves. The relationship we have with our bodies, our minds, and our spirit is the longest one we will have ever. When things get tough with others, we can always walk away. There is no way to ever walk away from yourself. We're stuck in this space and have to face our demons each day. Spending a lifetime mad at who we are, beating ourselves for our mistakes, or being ashamed of our failures will make for a very devastating existence.

Instead, envision a life where we have eternal mercy for our own journey. A relationship where we encourage ourselves and celebrate all of our minor victories. Do you have an age-old love with yourself, and mercy enough to remember that you're doing your best? How beautiful would that be every day?

Reflection Time

My friend take a few minutes to write all your minor victories. Take a few minutes to celebrate all the things you have done right, and all the things you have improved in the last couple weeks. Each thing you do should be subject to celebration and something to be proud of.

DAY 26

"There is no fear in love, but perfect love drives out fear because fear has to do with punishment, and so one who fears is not yet perfect in love. We love because he first loved us." (1 John 4:18-19)

Today, let us spend some time thinking of the concept of fear when it applies to love. Fear is a strong, and sometimes overwhelming, emotion. Many things can trigger our fears. They can be real or even imaginary. Many people are afraid to love for the fear of getting hurt, fear of being disappointed, or even the fear of losing their object of desire. This fear will hold people back from pursuing their dreams since they're so focused on the negative emotions.

Now, what if we let go of the fear? In today's scriptures, they remind us that perfect love has No Fear. The primary reason is because love, like us, comes from God. God's love is perfect. He fears nothing, and in terms gives us love freely and purely. God isn't sitting in heaven worried he will get his heart broken because we might not love him back. He just loves.

This is a type of love we are asked to have. A love so deep that it's not afraid of anything. The love that believes in us and is open to all. The first step is to face the fears holding us back and set them aside. Nobody can take away your love because you give it freely and without expectations.

Reflection Time

Have you ever considered that your fears are holding you back from being happy? If this is a new concept for you, take a few minutes to explore it. Then write a list of those potential fears that might hold you back and some ideas about how you can address them.

DAY 27

"For you love all things that are and loathe nothing that you have made; for what you hated, you would not have fashioned. And how could a thing remain, unless you willed it; or be preserved, had it not been called forth by you?" (Wisdom 11:24-25)

In 2012, they diagnosed me with thyroid cancer. Anytime somebody gives you a diagnosis with the C word, it turns your life upside down. That happened to me. And the words "*we found cancer in the thyroid*" brought me to my knees. Without wanting to, as soon as I hung up the phone, I started crying. It took me a couple of weeks to process everything that was happening, and by the grace of God, I was blessed with a brilliant doctor.

My doctors had a plan and were extremely confident everything was going to turn out fine. My mind understood the process, but I was still afraid and overwhelmed. I had a Catholic Bible that was given to me a few years earlier. I turned to it to find something that would give me strength. In the book of Wisdom—one of the few books found only in Catholic bibles—there was this scripture that became my new mantra. A prayer to God.

I focused on the fact that the Lord created me, unlike the cancer. Because of the love God had for me, he would destroy those cancer cells. Since he did not bring them into existence, there was no reason for them to stay in my body. That's how much love God has for us. It is our decision whether we put faith in this love. Life will always be a series of decisions. We determine which way we go.

Reflection Time

My friend, it is easy to put our faith in our fears. Primarily because placing our faith in things we cannot see is extremely hard. What I'm asking you to do today is to write the things that help you have faith in love. Take the time to truly ask yourself what is holding you back from loving freely.

DAY 28

"But God proves his love for us in that while we were still sinners Christ die for us." (Romans 5:8)

On day fourteen we talked about the greatest love to have, to give up our lives for one of our friends. Today's scripture, God is proving this concept for us. We must all remember that Jesus came to earth to show the people how to love. The Holy Trinity (the father, the son, and the Holy Spirit) want to have a relationship with us. To show us how life can be lived to the max when we fill it with love.

The Lord showed how much He loved his people by giving his only son to them to die. That, my friend, is the ultimate level of love. We don't have to be worthy of it. It's God's grace that gives us everything and showers us with blessings. Our job is to receive it. Don't run away from His blessing but give thanks for all of His glory.

The Lord sees our souls and intentions and loves us always. He's waiting for us with open arms for us to love him back. When we can love ourselves with all of our faults, we will be able to love others. When we accept who we are and accept God's love, loving others and those around us becomes a natural progression.

Reflection Time

Can you take a couple moments today to think of the times in your lives where you were blessed by God's love? Don't be afraid to explore those moments and truly find yourself as a loving creation.

CONGRATULATIONS MY FRIEND!

We have completed our fourth week together and have come to the end of our journey. I pray this devotional has been as fulfilling and empowering for you as it was for me. During our weeks together, we focused on the need to love not only others but ourselves. Love is more than just a powerful emotion; it comes with action steps to treat others and ourselves. As Paul explains, love is patient, love is kind, love forgives us, love endures all.

We are perfectly and abundantly made to express love to everyone we meet. Understanding that power gives us freedom to enjoy our lives more. Unconditional love can be scary if we've never seen it modeled around us. But it is not impossible. We can be the first ones in our families to live those principles and share them with others. Don't be afraid to take those steps of faith.

Always remember, my friend, that you are blessed and highly favored. The Lord wants you to have an incredible future full of joy and peace. You are not alone on this journey. He walks with you always. Thank you for allowing me to be a part of this journey with you and welcoming me into your home. It has truly been an honor to spend these four weeks with you.

Week 4 – Reflection Time

My friend, as you get ready to wrap up this devotional, take a few minutes to analyze your progress and reflect on all the changes you made during these four weeks. Take some time to see the beauty of love and how it can impact your life. Love can be a very scary and challenging thing to experience, but it is also one of the greatest blessings of our lives. Enjoy it, my friend.

ACKNOWLEDGEMENTS

It takes a village to create a book. I'm extremely grateful to all the members of my tribe who poured their hearts into this book with me.

This devotional would not have been possible without the incredible Ms. Cassandra Fear. Not only is she an incredible writer, she is an amazing editor and cover designer. Thank you so much, sweetie, for both editing and creating the cover for this book.

Thank you to the fabulous Ms. Kayla L. Wilkinson for becoming part of my tribe and adding your skills to polishing my books. So appreciate you!

My deepest thanks go to the talented Ms. Courtney Shockey for making my words look amazing on the page. Her patience with me is always incredible.

Thank you to my family for always believing in my dreams, even when they seem too far to reach.

Above all, my love and thanks go to you, my dear friends. Thank you for allowing me to be a part of this journey with you. I believe in you, and I believe you are destined for amazing things.

www.ingramcontent.com/pod-product-compliance
Lightning Source LLC
Chambersburg PA
CBHW071421040426
42445CB00012BA/1248
* 9 7 8 1 7 3 3 3 1 6 0 7 1 *